Hide-and-Seek Visual Adventures

UNCOVER NATURE

Published in 2010 by Windmill Books, LLC
303 Park Avenue South, Suite 1280
New York, NY 10010-3657

First published in 2009 by Orpheus Books Ltd.,
6 Church Green, Witney, Oxfordshire, OX28 4AW

Created and produced by Nicholas Harris, Sarah Hartley, Erica Williams, and Katie Sexton
Orpheus Books Ltd.

Illustrated by Studio Inklink

Text by Olivia Brookes

Library of Congress Cataloging-in-Publication Data

Brookes, Olivia.
Uncover nature / [text by Olivia Brooks] ; illustrated by Studio Inklink.
p. cm. -- (Hide-and-seek visual adventures)
Includes bibliographical references and index.
ISBN 978-1-60754-655-9 (library binding : alk. paper)
1. Nature--Juvenile literature. I. Title.

QH48.H327 2010
590--dc22
2009032540

Printed and bound in China

CPSIA compliance information: Batch # OR9002019: For further information contact Windmill Books, New York, New York at 1-866-478-0556.

Hide-and-Seek Visual Adventures

UNCOVER NATURE

Illustrated by Studio Inklink

an imprint of
WINDMILL BOOKS™

Contents

Introduction

Wherever you go on Earth, you'll find living things. From sweltering rainforests to icy Antarctica, from dusty deserts to the depths of the ocean, our planet teems with life: mammals, reptiles, birds, fish, insects, and plants. In this book, you can read about some interesting animals that live in different environments. Notice how the way they live their lives is perfectly suited to their surroundings. A penguin's thick feathers keep it warm as it goes hunting for fish in freezing polar waters— but it would quickly overheat in the jungle. A lazy sloth would struggle to find a branch to hang upside down from in the tree-less desert. And how would an elephant like living in the ocean?

Look out for the gold coin. One is hidden in each scene...

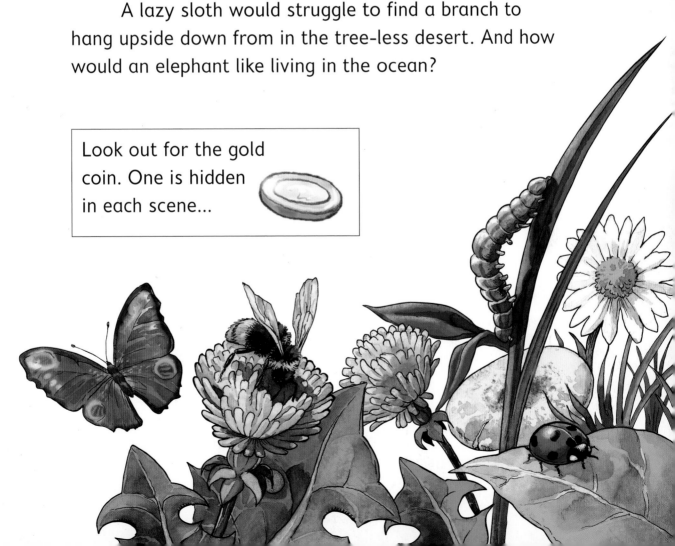

Rain Forest

Many different kinds of plants and animals live in tropical rain forests. It is hot and wet here all year round. Brightly colored butterflies flit through the trees and beautiful wading birds fish in the river.

Anacondas and crocodiles lurk close to the water's edge, waiting for their prey. High in the treetops, macaws and other birds squawk loudly, while monkeys leap from branch to branch. Most of the animals that live high in the trees will hardly ever touch the ground.

Turtle

Anaconda

Caiman

Piranha

Jaguar

Ants

Morpho butterfly

Hyacinth macaws are endangered birds. Prized as pets, many are captured for sale. In the wild, macaws nest in holes high up in tree trunks. They crack open nuts using their powerful bills.

The poison dart frog is so named because some Amazon natives use its deadly poison on the tips of their blow-gun darts. The frog gets its poison from the ants it eats.

The anaconda spends much of its time wallowing in shallow water waiting for its prey. It coils its body around its victim and squeezes it to death. Then it swallows it whole.

Macaw

Sloth

Squirrel monkey

Tree snake

Spider monkey

Bats

Deer

Tapir

Howler monkey

Humming-bird

Scarlet ibis

Poison dart frog

Iguana

Piranhas have razor-sharp, triangular teeth. Once they detect blood in the water, piranhas will set about an injured animal in a "feeding frenzy." In just a few minutes, all that's left is a skeleton!

A leaf-eater, the sloth spends most of its life hanging upside down. It grips on to branches with its long, hooked claws.

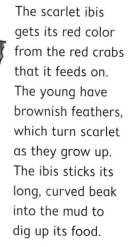

The scarlet ibis gets its red color from the red crabs that it feeds on. The young have brownish feathers, which turn scarlet as they grow up. The ibis sticks its long, curved beak into the mud to dig up its food.

Desert

Deserts are areas of land that have very little rain. This is the desert in the southwestern USA. During the day, temperatures can soar to more than 120°F (50°C).

Burrowing owl

Gila woodpecker

Roadrunner

Peccary

Skunk

Saguaro cactus

Kangaroo rat

Jackrabbit

Tarantula

Horned lizard

The horned lizard can squirt blood from the corner of its eyes to scare away attackers. It can also inflate its spiny body up to twice its size.

Peccaries are related to pigs. They have bristly hair and long, pointy teeth. They give off a strong odor so that other members of their herd can recognize each other. Using their sensitive snouts, they search the ground for grasses and roots.

The male burrowing owl prepares the burrow inside a cactus for the female. He stands guard at the entrance to scare away predators.

The saguaro cactus collects water from dew or rain and stores it in its thick stem. Many animals, including the kangaroo rat and the sidewinder snake, avoid the scorching heat by hiding in burrows or under rocks during the day.

Golden eagle

Deer

Peccary

Sidewinder

Gila monster

Scorpion

Tarantulas spend most of the time under the ground. They sit by the entrance to their burrow at night and wait for insects and other small animals to approach before pouncing on them.

The scorpion uses its pincers to grab its prey, such as an insect or small mammal. The stinger at the tip of its tail injects poison into it, making its victim unable to move. The scorpion then feasts on it.

Roadrunners prefer sprinting to flying, although they might take flight to escape coyotes. They can run at speeds of 15 mph, fast enough to snatch insects in mid-flight.

Savanna

During the dry season, the African savanna grasslands are hot and dusty. Animals gather at a watering hole to drink and cool down. Many plant-eating animals, such as zebras, antelopes, or gazelles, graze in herds. They must always be on the lookout for hungry predators, such as lions, cheetahs, and hyenas. Vultures are scavengers—they eat the remains of animals killed by others. They circle in the air, looking for leftovers to feed on.

Ostrich

Termites' nest

Zebra

Gazelle

Antelope

Rhinoceros

Giraffes are the tallest animals in the world. They use their long necks to feed on leaves and shoots from the treetops. They have excellent eyesight and can run at more than 30 mph (50 km/h)

Lions live together in prides of up to three males and 15 females. Lionesses do most of the hunting. They stalk zebra, antelope, and gazelle.

The zebra's black and white stripes are most likely a way of confusing predators. The patterns are unique to each zebra.

Vulture

Giraffe

Wildebeests

Elephant

Hippopotamus

Warthog

Hyena

Lion

Agama

The rhinoceros's huge body is covered with very thick skin. Its horns are made of a hard material that is similar to that found in fingernails.

The spotted hyena is a ferocious meat-eater. Its strong jaws can crush even bones and hooves. It may hunt large prey after a long chase, or scavenge kills made by other animals

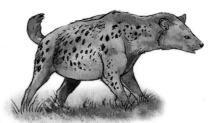

The African elephant is the largest of all land animals. Its trunk is really a nose and top lip combined. It is used to pick up food such as grass, leaves, branches, and fruit. It can also suck up water.

Coral Reef

Coral is made from the skeletons of tiny animals called polyps. They live together in large numbers. In shallow, sunlit waters in the tropics, huge banks of colorful coral, called reefs, build up near the seashore. Reefs are home to a large number of sea creatures. They feed on the tiny plants that float in the nearby waters. Large fish, such as barracudas, moray eels, and sharks feed on the smaller fish.

Barracuda

Turtle

Octopus

Moray eel

Starfish

Sea urchin

To stop themselves from being swept away in fast-flowing water, seahorses curl their long tails around sea grasses. Male seahorses carry the female's eggs in a special pouch before giving birth to the babies.

Starfish have neither heads nor brains. Their mouths are in the center of their bodies. Starfish creep slowly along the sea bed in search of their prey.

Octopuses have eight arms. They are probably the most intelligent of all invertebrates (animals without backbones). For defense, they can change color, or eject a cloud of ink to provide cover while they escape.

Seahorse

Jellyfish

Hammerhead
shark

Dolphin

Ray

Lionfish

Sea
anemone

Clownfish

Giant
clam

Hermit crab

Sea slug

The lionfish is protected by a fan of spiny fins. They are deadly to touch. Each fin contains enough venom to kill its prey of smaller fish.

A jellyfish's tentacles can sting or kill other animals. It drifts through the water feeding on small fish and other small marine creatures that become caught in these tentacles.

The eyes of a hammerhead shark are found on either side of its oddly shaped head. This dangerous animal can probably see all around it.

13

Antarctica

Antarctica is the coldest place on Earth. It is covered with thick ice all year round, although it only snows near the coast. The animals that live in Antarctica must be able to survive the freezing conditions.

Humpback whale

Crabeater seal

Humpback whales are called this because their backs curve when they dive. These huge whales are very acrobatic. They can leap high out of the water. This is called breaching.

When trying to attract a mate, a rockhopper penguin will shake its head to and fro, showing off its yellow feathers.

Crabeater seals do not actually eat crabs. Instead they eat tiny shrimp-like creatures called krill. They swim with their mouths wide open. The water drains away through their teeth, leaving behind the krill. Yummy!

Some have layers of fat, called blubber, under their skins to keep them warm. A penguin's dense mat of feathers keeps the cold water out and the warmth of its body in.

Albatross

Sperm whale

Elephant seals

Emperor penguins

Rockhopper penguin

After laying her egg, the female emperor penguin returns to the sea to feed. The male protects it on his feet for more than 60 days.

A sperm whale's head makes up a third of its body. The whales "call" to one other with clicks that can be heard several miles away. They are able to dive down more than 3000 feet in search of their favorite food, giant squid.

An albatross has a wingspan of up to 11.5 feet (3.5 m) more than any other bird. It can fly for hours, gliding on air currents, without having to flap its wings. Sometimes it swoops down to the surface to scoop up fish or squid.

Bald eagle

Bison

Moose

Grizzly bear

Lynx

Chipmunks

Wolverine

When a salmon jumps out of the water, on its way back to its breeding grounds upstream, a grizzly bear is there ready to catch it in its jaws or paws.

Male moose, or bulls, can grow antlers nearly six and a half feet across. They are designed to impress females and rivals in the autumn mating season.

Beavers can fell trees by gnawing them with their razor-sharp teeth. They use the fallen logs to dam a stream, making a lake around their lodge. This protects them from predators.

Forest

Dangerous predators prowl through the northern conifer forests. Wolves hunt in packs. They howl to let other wolves know where they are.

Though they are small, wolverines can kill animals that are bigger than they are. They sometimes kill more animals or scavenge more meat than they can eat, so they store the rest underground.

Crane

Otters

Beavers

Wolf

The bald eagle keeps a lookout for its prey while soaring in the air high above. It can spot fish more than half a mile away. It swoops down at great speed and then glides above the water before grabbing its victim in its feet and flying off to eat it.

Tufts of black hair sprout from the tips of a lynx's ears. These act as a hearing aid, helping the wild cat hear its prey from a long way off.

Cranes perform spectacular mating dances. They leap into the air with their wings outstretched and their feet forward. At the end of the dance, they even bow to one another!

Woodland

The woodlands come alive at night when many animals come out to eat or hunt for their prey. During the summer months, animals such as squirrels and rodents feed on

Jay

Green woodpecker

Roe deer

Woodcock

Hedgehog

Pheasant

Blackbird

The weasel is a slim animal with a long tail and short legs. A ferocious little predator, it chases its prey, mice, voles, or rabbits, down their burrows. It is active both in the day and at night. A weasel might steal its burrow from one of its prey.

Woodpeckers uses their claws to grip onto tree trunks. There, they hammer into the bark with their long beaks to find insects to eat or to dig out nesting holes.

The red fox gives birth to its cubs in the spring. An average litter is five cubs. The young are born blind and cannot open their eyes until they are about two weeks old.

fruit and nuts from the trees. In the winter, food is harder to find. The trees lose their leaves and many birds migrate, or fly away to warmer lands. Some animals hibernate until spring.

Blue tit

Squirrels

Badgers

Rabbits

Weasel

Dormouse

Foxes

Only the male roe deer has antlers. During the rut (breeding season), the male, or buck, rubs them against the barks of trees to mark out his territory. Bucks fight each other to mate with females, called does.

Badgers can dig a maze of underground chambers and tunnels called a sett. Badger cubs can be seen near the entrances to their home playing and pretending to fight.

Hedgehogs have prickly spines everywhere except their face, legs, and bellies. To protect themselves from predators, they curl up into a tight ball. They sniff around looking for slugs, snails, beetles, and earthworms.

Woodland Floor

They might be hard to spot, but many small creatures live under the ground. For example, ants make their homes in underground nests. They live together in large groups called colonies. In each colony, there is a queen ant who is looked after by thousands of worker ants.

Bees also live in large colonies. Worker bees use their long tongues to collect nectar from flowers. They take it back to their nests to make into honey.

Rabbits

Bee

Snail

Ants

As a mole digs, it pushes the earth up to the surface to form molehills. Earthworms are its favorite food. The mole bites the heads off first and saves the rest for later.

Earthworms are made up of many small segments. Each is covered in tiny hairs that grip the soil. This allows the worm to pull itself along.

The ladybug is a kind of beetle. Its bright colors and markings are a warning to predators that it tastes bad. When disturbed, the ladybug produces tiny amounts of foul-smelling yellow blood from its legs.

Beetle

Woodlice

Spider

Butterfly

Mole

Caterpillar

Earthworm

Centipede

Slug

Ladybird

Spiders use their webs to catch their prey. Any insect that flies into a web gets caught in its sticky strands. The spider paralyzes it with its venom then wraps it up in silk, for eating later.

Some butterflies have markings on their wings that look like large eyes. Attackers are fooled into thinking the eyes belong to a larger animal, and are scared off.

Rabbits dig a series of burrows, called a warren, where they sleep and tend to their young. They are also a place to escape from predators.

Index

Did you find them?

pages 6-7

pages 8-9

pages 10-11

pages 12-13

pages 14-15

pages 16-17

pages 18-19

pages 20-21

For more great fiction and nonfiction, go to www.windmillbooks.com